life is a

disappearing

act

life is a
disappearing
act

Ron Wallace

Text copyright © 2024 by Ron Wallace
All Rights Reserved. Printed in the United States of America

Published by Motina Books, LLC, Van Alstyne, Texas
www.MotinaBooks.com

Library of Congress Cataloguing-in-Publication Data:

Names: Wallace, Ron
Title: Life Is a Disappearing Act::New and Collected Poems
Description: First Edition. | Van Alstyne: Motina Books, 2024

Identifiers:

LCCN: 2023951521

ISBN-13: 979-8-88784-030-7 (paperback)
ISBN-13: 979-8-88784-031-4 (hardcover)
ISBN-13: 979-8-88784-033-8 (audiobook)
ISBN-13: 979-8-88784-032-1 (e-book)

Subjects: BISAC:
POETRY / American / General

For Terry Ray Risner, my very first nephew, my little brother:

You may have disappeared from this swiftly spinning rock, but in my heart, you will always be.

People leave and they never come back.
Life is a disappearing act.
~ *Gretchen Peters*

In Ron Wallace's first book, *Native Son*, my father wrote in the introduction that he'd love to take even the slightest credit for making Ron a poet, but he couldn't. He also said Howard Starks and James Dickey could claim powerful influences, but after ten volumes of poetry, I think Ron would agree there is a piece of Dennis Letts in there. My father and mother both have written introductions to his works. They called his writing "powerful, and beautiful, and sensual, and absolutely honest". Now his new collection echoes those sentiments, and I know Mom and Dad would be proud.

Tracy Letts
Author of *The Man from Nebraska*
(2004 Pulitzer Prize finalist) and
August Osage County
(2008 Pulitzer Prize winner)

An icon of Oklahoma poetry comes calling on our attention again, asking us to ponder the shadow outlines others leave behind, how we fill them in, how we define what we will leave behind in turn. In this collection of new and collected poems, Wallace re-shares older wisdom (because sometimes we don't listen the first time) and offers up new wisdom (because sometimes we do). The leaves within this collection are autumnal and haunting, but there is also the warmth of Spring lurking among them, like his father's "got away with it grin" Wallace pockets at the close of the opening poem.

Paul Juhasz
Author of *The Inner Life of Comics*
Director of the Woody Guthrie Poets

INTRODUCTION

Ron Wallace begins his new book *Life Is a Disappearing Act* with a quote from the singer/songwriter Gretchen Peters: "People leave, and they never come back. Life is a disappearing act." While Ron acknowledges this simple fact, the eventual loss of parents, a "little brother," a beloved dog, and everyday moments that slowly fade from memory, he performs the artist's sleight of hand, bringing them back for us to share. Like his father who, in the poem "Leaving Oakland 1944," chooses at the end of World War II to return to Oklahoma "just above the Red River" because "home for him is anywhere with" (his beloved wife, Ron's mother). Ron too has chosen this place, a constant in his life and his poetry, a place that "in these tired rain-soaked December days" we come to witness in ways we may never have understood before.

In this volume of collected and new poems, we revisit familiar themes from Ron's previous ten books. Too often collected poems arrive with little coherence from writers whose skills are slowly eroding but who may, through this process, claim they are not yet letting go. That is not the case with this fine collection before you. The poems Ron has selected from five of his previous books have been chosen with a deft sense of how they cohere, how they fit with extraordinary new poems, including "What I Took," "Approaching Seventy," "Leaving Oakland 1944," and "Two Men" which are among the best that Ron Wallace has given us.

As with the poetry of B. J. Fairchild, a poet Ron greatly admires, these poems make us wish to be worthy of a place where "bones lie . . . stilled by this ever-fatal falling of leaves." As in this poem "Comes November" about his beloved dog Gandalf, when Ron says, "I have not forgotten you," he is also speaking of us and of this place where he has chosen to live the whole of his life.

"I am only air whistling in through one open window of a 1971 forest-green Mercury Cougar then out the other, invisible and unseen, blowing plastic Walmart bags up into the air to tumble from the perfect blue of Oklahoma like broken kites falling from grace," concludes the poem "Approaching Seventy." And so, we are blessed with these lovely narrative pieces that Ron, whose poems never fall from grace, is compelled to write.

Markham Johnson
Author of *Dear Dreamland*
Winner of the Pablo Neruda Poetry Prize

WHAT I TOOK / 1

COMES NOVEMBER / 2

APPROACHING SEVENTY / 6

SEPTEMBER ENDING / 8

CRASH / 9

RUNNING / 10

AUGUST ENDING / 12

COMPLICIT / 13

GHOSTS / 14

THE COMPANY I KEEP / 16

FIREFALL / 18

COMES WINTER TO THE NIGHT / 19

SAME STARS / 20

TWO MEN / 22

FRAGILE / 23

LEARNING TO SPEAK CHOCTAW / 24

LEAVING OAKLAND 1944 / 26

UNRAVELING / 27

TYGER / 28

ON A BUS TO BROKEN BOW / 30

IN MY FATHER'S BOOKS / 32

MOTHER'S TOUCH / 33

ALL I KNOW / 34

HANK / 36

HOUSE PAINTING 101 / 37

THE WAY OF THE BUFFALO / 40

HOW THE HELL DID I GET HERE / 41

LETTING GO / 42

MICKEY MANTLE AND CHINABERRY TREES / 44

A FEW THINGS I'VE COME TO KNOW / 46

THE COWBOY RIDES AWAY / 47

WHAT I TOOK

After you were gone,
        I went back home
one more time.
I looked at the vacant recliner,
the television screen empty of John Wayne,
the curtains drawn closed on every window.
I took the books I'd given you
        mostly westerns
        mostly Louis L'Amour.
I took a neatly penciled grocery list
you'd written on the back
        of an old receipt.
I took the walking stick you had carved
from a hardwood limb
        your cowboy hat,
and half a bottle of Old Spice after shave.
I walked out to your elm-tree shade
and sat a while
        until the sun began to set
behind the peanut mill across the road.
I breathed in the last air of October,
holding your Captain's Badge
in my right hand
and made a promise I will always keep.
Then,
with the first coming of stars,
I took your got-away-with-something grin
tucked it in my pocket
        for another day,
                pulled on your old hat
                        climbed in my Jeep
                                and drove away.

COMES NOVEMBER

Outside my window, October lies
      defeated, broken,
awaiting the cold.

The grey sky has buried the blue
      beneath a chill rain,
and the lawn is lost in leaves,
dampened by this christening of autumn.

Among the hickory, blackjack oak and American elm,
I walk where leaves are falling
      reluctant to surrender summer,
a futile resistance to the impending close of seasons.

I find you beneath the overhang of short roof
      near our southern door
           on your much-loved, worn-out blanket.
My hand falls to your head
and scratches between your standing ears
as you try to rise and meet me
      one more time.

But you cannot.

Your strength is gone
      so we sit,
your head, resting on my folded legs,
where I speak soft words
until you look up, right into my eyes,
offering a sad apology for a warrior's weakness.

We have only this moment,
and just before your dark eyes close a final time
        with a soft exhale of October air,
I see my face,
my own eyes, reflected in yours
        and I know
that a part of me will walk with you
into the coming of winter.

Twenty Octobers have faded since
into twenty Novembers,
        into twenty winters,
and those slowly falling leaves have come again.
I can feel the not-too-distant cold
pulsing in the ache of stiff knuckles.

Outside,
among the golden browns, I walk
startling a handful of raucous crows
        who burst and blow away
while two grey squirrels
dart from limb to limb above my path
        to this spot
where I come to find you,
a once perfect symmetry of lines,
a graceful, fluid movement of muscles and tendons
        that always stood with me.
Your bones lie here,
stilled by this ever-fatal falling of leaves.

But, I have not forgotten you.

Beyond our western hills,
I sense December's shadow
        coming to swallow shorter suns,
and my fingers recall soft fur, black on tan.
I sit back on boot heels
        to brush away leaves,
covering a cinder block that marks your grave

where you lie, keeping my reflection,
in closed brown eyes.

Once more
I speak in soft tones,
telling you of the squirrels that you would chase,
the golden leaves you would race among,
     and as always,
          I sense your rising
and know you hold me
in those dark eyes
     as I have kept you in mine.

And for just a brief flickering,
we will walk winter's edge together,
before I let you rest
     to await my return again.

APPROACHING SEVENTY

As my sixty-ninth summer fades,
I wander out to the rim of the world
        and wonder,
What brought me here?
        Which god rolled the dice?
                Who wove this tangled web?
Was it the consequence of unplanned circumstance
        or the mere vagaries of fate?

Should I have been another poet like Hank Williams
        a lightning bolt
that lit a pitch-black night
before fading
        into a cold and lonely New Year's sky?

I suppose not.
I have somehow evaded the siren's call
        of pills and alcohol
and managed to avoid the backseats
of haunted Cadillacs.

I guess
I could have been
any one of those ten thousand dead draftees
lost in the unholy jungles of Vietnam,
        unsung and unknown
except for names carved in a wall of jet-black stone,
but my eighteenth birthday fell
in the later numbers
        of a dead man's lottery.

Instead,
I have found these tired
      rain-soaked December days
      where I am only air
         whistling
in through one open window
of a 1971 forest-green Mercury Cougar
      then out the other
invisible and unseen,
blowing plastic Walmart bags
      up into the air
         to tumble
from the perfect blue of Oklahoma
like broken kites.

SEPTEMBER ENDING

Summer crosses the green field
in a crawl
    of black cattle,
ambling with low guttural moans,
and the night call of crickets
    far dimmer than only days ago
evoking a sadness
buried inside, deeper than my days.

In the stillness
of this clove of seasons,
somewhere
beyond the depth of my eyes
    an owl takes wing
from tangled trees,
invisible
    silent,
a lover's whisper of goodbye
fading like falling leaves
as the world's shadow shifts
    beneath his wings
        and falls
across the colors of an autumn night.

Light leaves,
time pours into a new moon,
and the final fireflies of summer
steal the darkness from Orion's belt
as I watch the nothing
    that they are becoming.

CRASH

Sometimes
I can still see that yellow tennis ball
        bouncing
                in high golden arcs
down the steep slant of green shingles,
where I have flung it.
The sun rising with each rebound
        setting with each descent.

I stalk its every leap from the green
        measuring its angle
                its speed
                        its shifting path,
never knowing that in truth, it is stalking me.

Timing is everything.

If it strikes near the edge of eaves
        its crescent is smooth and easily gloved,
but if it clears the edge of everything,
to prevent the collision of sun and earth,
I must dive
        extending
the entire length of my frame
and strike the earth like a meteor
        then rise
and fire the yellow back higher into the blue,
life rising, descending
        rising, descending
                rising, descending
until the ultimate final crash of body and dirt.

RUNNING

In dreams I drive the ball
      above the glove
of a leaping second baseman
toward the gap in right-center.
      And I separate
in midstride
from the wood, polished smooth
from a thousand swings
and made tacky with pine tar.

I feel thighs flex,
feel my calves become pistons
      as I round first
          no hesitation,
dark hair flying like a battle flag
in a cavalryman's charge.

And as if I am viewing this all on film,
I watch the outfielder
cut the ball
      plant
          pivot,
and fire the leather pellet
toward the base where I am diving
      headfirst
          hard,
a cloud of red clay dust rising
to obscure the black 15 on my back
before a soundless collision
      of flesh and bone
echoes in the silence of sleep.

In dreams,
        just like in life,
I never hit the ball over the wall
and trot like Mickey Mantle
first to home.
No.
I always have to run.
I run
from tigers
        or wolves
                or myself.

But this is a dream game,
and when I stand from the crash
        inexplicably
                in dream fashion,
I am standing,
not on second base but
one foot
        on third,
                out of oxygen
tagging up to make a mad dash
for home
as the bone white sphere
        floats
                toward left,
                        shallow,
too shallow to give me any chance
but regardless,
I know I will run.

In dreams I always run.

AUGUST ENDING

The last days of August hum
a September song
    through the leaves
        an elegy
of cicadas
whispered on wings over grass
    still green,
above the last fireflies
    dancing,
in the dying light of summer.

The days are still catching fire,
and the cold is distant yet,
but I can feel the earth
    begin its long,
        slow turn
           toward winter.
And I can sense the shortness of days
moving toward me,
here in this anthracite night
    each setting sun
        falling on the quiet feathers
of the great horned owl
who haunts my November nights
    bringing winter.

COMPLICIT

I am the son of a cop
      a good man
who taught me to look past the badge
and beyond the uniform
      to see the human heart
that beats inside all men.
I was brought to understand
      that justice denied
leads to a nation laid to waste,
and I must never be complicit.
      But now,
I walk among bastards
who play by the same rules that govern piranhas
      men who lead
with the same ego as Custer
riding ahead of the Seventh Cavalry.
These men
      however,
will not fall with those they lead
      These men
would burn Greenwood to the ground again
and go to church that next Sunday
believing God is on their side.
They lack compassion
        courage
           remorse,
but not stockpiles of ammunition.
Given the opportunity,
these men would devour the world
      swallow it whole
        and spit out the bones.

GHOSTS

With Jackson Browne
playing sad and soft on my stereo.
I turn the volume down just a notch,
push repeat
      and step out onto my deck
where I can settle into the sunset
like a ghost.

A bottle of good bourbon whiskey
      a glass of ice cubes,
and the sound of the wind
leaving me alone,
I watch the night's first stars
      break the black.

The last light of May is gone in shadows.

Beneath these trees that know me well
I pull up a chair and sit
to watch summer drip
      from a bone-white moon
            through hard, scarred bark
and leaves painted black by falling night.

How many shades of black exist
in a night like this?
      Hundreds?
            Thousands?
                  Maybe more?

I seek the answers
　　　in four fingers more,
poured over what little ice remains,
then seal the bottle
　　　like a love letter's envelope
　　　　　and lift a toast,
to summon the other ghosts
who dwell in darkness.

And if the music and the whiskey
　　　are just about right,
most likely
one of my many phantoms will step out
and sit with me a while.

The slate grey
will mingle with the little slivers of light
　　　creating intricate patterns
between the pitch of elms and oaks
on a sky
　　　darker
than all the holes in the world
and I can step off the edge
　　　and disappear.

THE COMPANY I KEEP

My lawn lies in three feet of leaves
fallen from oak and elm
      to gather in multitudes
          unnumbered
as fall turns into a warm winter.

From beneath a sweat-stained
      Stetson brim,
my eyes survey ground,
buried beneath an autumn avalanche
that I intend to move
      into drifts
piling them atop the wind-crashed pine
and lightning-shattered hackberry.

Clad in the bright blue of a Jimmy Buffett tee
      the well-worn,
faded denim of Wrangler jeans,
and a pair of boots beaten into submission,
I drive dead leaves
      from a rocky drainage ditch
toward their resting place
as field mice scurry for more cover.

Unbothered by the activity,
a young redtail lands
in the barren branches of a mimosa tree.
He has come to hunt
the mice that I uncover from hidden nests
      or any other game,
foolhardy enough to show itself
while he waits in camouflage.

I know
some may think him cruel
when he strikes
            with sudden damage,
but he is the company I keep,
        survivor,
taloned predator,
mottled in colors of tree and leaf.

FIREFALL

Beneath the prairie's summer ceiling
a star falls
      blazing
across a blackened field of night
      then disappears
            in a sudden arc.

How long had that light
burned white in the dark ocean above?

Infinite herds of Oklahoma bison once
roamed below its flicker.
Hunting Horse and Teddy Roosevelt slept
beneath its shimmer
      before a thousand cities
rose like blades of grass under its light.

And now
      like a forgotten dream
          it is gone.
But still, even in its absence
      the symmetry of the sky
is pleasing to the eye.
Other stars still burn in the night,
      as bright as before.
Nonetheless,
change has come
      and night
          will never be
          exactly
as it used to be,
ever again.

COMES WINTER TO THE NIGHT

Darkness comes
screaming like a panther,
and all the gods that I have abandoned
      gather in small falling flakes
calling me to the night outside the window glass,
where they swallow the streetlight
      and burn into white ash
on the cold ground.

In the dark and starless December sky
      days dance
through sixty some odd seasons
like drunken half breeds
and hang like tinsel on a discarded tree.

I believe
this is how some things are meant to end,
not with Eliot's whimper
      but a sudden gust of icy wind,
head thrown back and howling,
blowing darkened light below the rattle
of black branches
      sweeping stars into crystal drifts
to be buried in winter
beneath a distant dirge of haunted highland pipes.

SAME STARS

Above the ragged black of the Mississippi
      beyond the reach
of New Orleans lights,
I watch stars
      hang above the water
carrying their light to the Gulf of Mexico.

Ancient astronomers
named these same stars
      Orion, Hercules, Callisto
Perseus, and the ploughman.
Ten thousand poets have recorded
      the shattering of the black
when constellations unfolded
among the heavens,
and countless lovers
      have lain beneath them,
making wishes that seldom came true.

These are the same stars
that have shone
      for centuries in our world,
the same stars
that Crockett watched from the walls
of the Alamo.
They are the same stars
      my father slept out under
when he rode the rails to California,
and the same stars my mother counted
      every night
until he returned to her and Oklahoma.

They are the same stars
        that I have followed
on unnumbered and unnamed roads
across the land of coyotes
and Cochise
        over mountains and rivers
to look into the Grand Canyon,
or watch the sun set on Abbey's Arches.
These are the same stars
that light the Alabama grave of Hank Williams.
They are the same stars made invisible
by Time Square lights
        the same stars
that crown the Wind River Range
before they flicker above the Little Big Horn.

They are the same stars
that I have followed home again and again
        from the coast of Oregon
                    the peaks of Colorado,
the deserts of Arizona and New Mexico
        the same stars
that followed me
from the bleacher seats of Yankee Stadium
        to the shores of Carolina
            and Memphis, Tennessee.

So, standing here, tonight
        how
can I not wonder
if somewhere out there,
in the mountains so far away,
these same stars
        are being watched by you
as they flicker into view, one by one.

TWO MEN

Two men, looking like
they just stepped straight out of a Steinbeck novel
      stand, posing for the depression
      as poor as Oklahoma
but as solid as the steel rails they stand on.

The big man on the left
      smiling a sad Okie smile
      with his big cowboy hat pushed back
is my Uncle Ira.

The shorter man
standing shoulder to shoulder with him,
wearing a hat looking like Henry Fonda
      playing Tom Joad,
           is my father.

The photo is fading.

Time has eaten their legs from the knees down
and once black and white shades
      of green and blue behind them
          are now undefined,
              disappearing,
making them seem to rise from the earth.

Almost a century has faded into grey
      just like the photograph,
and I am nearing seventy,
twice their age when time froze them
      in Kodak paper,
but my boots still embrace this dirt,
this Oklahoma,
because their bones lie beneath it.

FRAGILE

Most of us
live in a world
where dragons are kept outside the fence
      only
by two rusted iron chains
woven together
with a single strand of baling wire
      a gate
            fashioned
by some old cowboy
who lived
      long before
we ever came into existence.

LEARNING TO SPEAK CHOCTAW

He rose like smoke from high grass
that had taken the alley
     east of the Katy tracks
and shuffled across the gravel road,
black hair, dark eyes
     a hundred creases
in his dark brown, leathered face.

His brown hand lifted
as he saw my father bent under the hood
of his old red Chevy.

"Halito, Leonard Wallace, chim achukma?"

His long sleeves pulled his hands back inside
khaki pockets.

Dad's head remained in the motor.
"Hello Earl, I'm fine.
How are you this morning, need a ride?"

"Jus' walkin', Captain.
Headed for Red's, get me a hamburger
     if you spot me a quarter,
jus' 'til I mow me a few lawns."

I stopped bouncing the ball off the shed,
eyed the worn brogans on his feet,
and glanced at Dad still buried in his Chevy.

The old man looked at me and my beat up ball glove.

"Halito, Little Wallace,
     you the next Allie Reynolds?"

I shrugged
        he grinned.

"Keep throwin' that ball, you be another Super Chief."

Dad finally came out of the engine
pulled a handful of silver
and flipped a quarter to the old Choctaw.

He caught the coin with ease.

"Yokoke, my policeman friend,
I owe you four quarters
        I know.
                I go eat, now."

He moved like tall grass in an easy wind,
up the gravel road to the railroad track
        and out of sight,
my eyes following in his wake.

"War and wine,
goddamned war and wine,"
        Dad melted back into the motor,
me, standing dumb and silent as a post.

"Throw the ball, son
        just keep throwing that ball."

LEAVING OAKLAND 1944

It was my father's favorite photograph.
The two of them stand
          before green-leaved vines
near the bay, on the western wall of California,
a war winding down
          no more ships to build
                    no more reason to stay.

Both have west-coast Okie sisters rooted there
          but home for her
lies just above Red River
where sunsets burn shades of rose and purple
and oceans sleep a thousand miles away.

Home for him is anywhere with her.

So the camera catches
her finally-leaving-California smile
          and a twinkle
in her Oklahoma grey eyes,
four small red stones set in silver
          hanging
from a sterling chain around her neck,
Dad pressed to her right side,
          coming home.

UNRAVELING

There are these times
when life bolts
from beneath me
     unexpected
and I feel like a bronc rider
thrown into an empty sky
     Icarus in a cowboy hat
plunging wingless
through the vacant blue of May
into a spiral
where all things
recede into nothingness,
     time unraveling
like the threadbare cuffs
of my favorite chambray shirt.

And in these times
I am certain
that if the tigers found Bukowski
     eventually
they will find me too.

When I have fears that I may cease to be
John Keats

TYGER

I have reached a place
where days drop like Greek soldiers
from the belly of a wooden horse.
And I try to unravel shards of memory
      hoping to understand
how I've come to be who I am,
the son of an Okie cop
      born into outlaw territory.

But I am not my father,
an unstoppable force of nature.

I am more my mother
who forged her own rules,
right or wrong in the eyes of others
      always right in hers.

Now, the road is ending,
and I sense an elemental gathering
of should-have-beens
      and might-have-beens
          signaling
the impending arrival of the never-will-bes.

And often on cold winter days
      just before dawn
I sense the eyes of Blake's Tyger
      flickering
      red against the black
      teeth gleaming.

I hear him padding out there on the periphery,
where he pauses like a specter
        on the edge of darkness
and beckons me to join him
in that void
where all things are swallowed
        and I,
I am sometimes tempted
to enter his shadow world
        step up
and place my hand gently on his fur.

ON A BUS TO BROKEN BOW

Thumbing through fractured pages
     yellowing,
in a used bookstore on Decatur Street
down in New Orleans,
I found an arcane marker holding a place
in an aging paperback from 1955.

A bus ticket from Texarkana
     to Broken Bow
lay fading between pages 58 and 59
where some forgotten reader
had closed the past
     and disappeared
          almost without a trace.

But the ghost had left
     a little piece of soul,
underlined in ink on a fragile page
with Jeffers' soft commands:

"Love your eyes that can see, your mind
that can hear the music, the thunder of the wings.
Love the wild swan."

I wondered
where the eyes that read those words
     the hands that held that pen,
the heart that felt
the thunder of those wings, had gone.

How did this brittle paperback
cross states and rivers to land on these shelves?
Was this fate?
Was I predestined to find these lines
        and carry them back?

Or was this merely chance
        a random act
ordained by a love of literature,
or perhaps a need
to step out of French Quarter heat?

No answers were unveiled
        no solutions unfolded.

Time and circumstance
        had turned the living blood
who rode a Greyhound bus into Oklahoma,
with poetry in their eyes
into a dusty puzzle
        too many pieces missing.

So, this is how it is in the end
        I suppose;
we all wind up as scraps of paper,
hidden in some forgotten spot
        question marks
in the hearts and minds of strangers
whom we will never know.

IN MY FATHER'S BOOKS

I found my father's stolen words
     his voice
carved in black pencil marks
on margined pages
     echoing
like a rifle shot through the trees.

I read the lines, underlined
     lines,
my father's once blue eyes
     faded grey
had held in the coming light of winter,
words that mattered
     burned into him.

Oils from his rough fingertips
     bled into these pages
where he scratched his thoughts,
marking his progress
     now spoke to me.

I felt him rise
     to live again,
here… in *Sackett's Brand.*
And with each page I turn
     he turns
back into denim and leather,
muscles made
swinging a nine-pound hammer
     flex
beneath khaki sleeves
and he walks away from the wreckage
     a cage of failing flesh
that tried to pen him in his final hours.

MOTHER'S TOUCH

Had you been born to a different time
      a different world,
you'd have been a painter
or perhaps a poet
      but fate placed you here,
an amethyst set in a silver brooch
that held us all together.

You were a fryer of chickens
      a maker of dolls,
a cultivator of flowers, trees, and grandchildren,
thriving in summer heat like
      some exotic blossom,
and with the coming of longer suns,
I sense roses, peonies, and mimosas flowering
into your smile.

You only hold me now
      in shades of black and white,
but I hold you in the vivid purples, reds, deep blues,
and bright greens all around me.
      I sense you
in the full moon and stars above me,
feel your mother's touch,
stroking my little boy hair with soft breezes
as I stand amid the sleeping flowers
      alone in the darkness
            that you taught me not to fear.

ALL I KNOW

Sometimes Life is the lightning strike
      beneath the thunderclap.
Sometimes it's the rain
that falls on quiet summer afternoons.
      Sometimes it's the curled kittens,
asleep in their mother's fur,
but more often it's the hunting hawk
      who rides the winter air.

Sometimes
Life is a devil
standing among the roses
      wearing a mask made of silk
to hide his wicked smile
and spurs of Spanish silver
      that jangle
when he rides the storm across the stars.

Life can walk on moonlight
to seek a woman's lips
      and whisper honeyed words
as sweet thighs wrap like iron
around your waist
      in songs of Stevie Nicks
and lines of soft blue tattoos.

Sometimes it needs all the answers
      Sometimes
It forbids any questions asked.

Life may come knocking,
dressed in a cowboy hat and heart attacks
        tearing down curtains
that you use to cloak your past.

Only one thing I know is certain:

Life never waits
        in comfort
                or recline.
It never ever slows its pace
for those who fall too far behind.

It simply
pulls on its high-topped boots,
buttons up its favorite chambray shirt,
tucks it in its worn and faded denim jeans
        before smoothing back its hanging hair
and rides away
without a single word of warning
or a second thought of consequence.

HANK

The first of all cats
        you rose
deep grey smoke floating
along the wooden rail through tangled roses.
        Heaven help
the neighbor's Doberman pup
who missed you, hidden in the camouflage
until you descended
        claws flashing
                sending him stumbling
in yelps of pain and terror.

Your constant ally,
I emerged to find you swaggering back
        like some old pirate
up the steps to greet me as if to say,
"No problem here, my man; it's all under control."

Then the rub between my leather boots
        in and out
        in and out
before I bend and lift you
victorious and stroke the scarred muscles
beneath gunmetal grey
        velvet on iron.

My notched-eared old warrior
        ragged and unconquered,
you are remembered fondly.
If not by the ghosts of roses and youthful canines
        then by me
standing in the darkness, here on your deck

HOUSE PAINTING 101

(For Sioux)

Balancing myself on the steel ladder
    I brush dark green paint
        on corner trim boards
and watched him reach into his shirt pocket
to retrieve a half empty pack
of Lucky Strike cigarettes.
He removed the sweat-stained Resistol straw,
placed it crown-down
    on a sawhorse,
and ran his fingers through iron grey hair.

"When you starting college, boy?
You ain't gonna paint houses or saw 2x4s
and hammer nails in planks your whole life
    are ya?"

Afraid to meet his eyes,
I focus on keeping the trim green
    and the boards white.
 "Maybe after next summer."

He pulled the crumpled cowboy hat back on,
poured the rolling tray full again,
soaked the long-handled roller brush
and started pushing ivory paint up the wall.

"Your momma and daddy want you in college
 this fall, boy."

I reach up to get the top of the trim,
and a drop of green plops on the curls
on my shoulder-length hair
and bleeds through to my Jerry Jeff Walker,
"Viva Terlingua" tee shirt.

"Damn it all to hell,"
I swear in my most manly voice.
"And I've had all the school shit I can stand,
        right now, at least."
An even more manly cursing of education,
I thought.

He lay the roller in the tray
and tapped another Lucky from the pack.

"Get your ass down, boy.
        Let's take a break
                drink us a cold pop."

He exhaled a cloud of smoke
and stubbed out a cigarette butt on the ground
with his sharp-toed cowboy boots.

"Look here, son,
you're wasting time doing this crap work."
He held up his left hand.
"Look at them fingers, boy.
        I beat every one of 'em flat
with a goddamn hammer over the years.
You think that was my game plan?
        Hell no,
I was gonna ride rodeo
saddle broncs in Calgary, Cheyenne
        Las Vegas,
not do this piddling shit my whole life."

I just sort of stared at the literally flat fingers and mumbled
something about wanting to play ball.

"Ball players and bronc riders get old, son.
If you don't get your butt in school soon, you never will.
You'll look up one day, and you'll be sixty-eight
        divorced twice,

whitewashing another man's walls,
driving a piece-of-shit-Chevy
        and smoking these death sticks."

It was the most he'd ever said to me in one sitting.

"I sure don't plan on doing this forever, Sioux."

He coughed and spat phlegm.
"Neither did I, son
        neither did I.
Turpentine'll take the paint outta your hair,
but that shirt ain't ever comin' clean."
I tried to see the bright green stain
out of the corner of my eye.

        He fired up another Lucky.
"I reckon there's a lotta pretty gals in that college.
Gals that don't care for paint
        all over a fella's clothes."

He chuckled.
"Better get back up on that ladder.
        We still got a wall and a half to go."

I enrolled that fall.

THE WAY OF THE BUFFALO

Too much of Oklahoma
has gone the way of the buffalo,
     faded
into ink-stained pages,
      forgotten
like old rodeo posters, long left behind.

Too much has disappeared
in falling sunsets,
buried like bones of bison
     beneath the native grass
or made into painted skulls
to hang
     on rich men's walls.

Claremore clings to Will Rogers,
     like a lost lover
holds on to hope,
while Okemah tries to reclaim
a trace of Woody Guthrie's ghost.

     James Garner
has turned ten foot tall and solid bronze
to stand alone in Norman.
But Quanah Parker is here no more.
He went away by halves
     first the red half
        then the white.
Jim Thorpe
     lies buried way up north
far from our plains and prairies,
and like his own creation
Ralph Ellison is near invisible now.

Too much of Oklahoma is gone.

HOW THE HELL DID I GET HERE

How the hell did I get here,
here to this blue ending of summer?

When last I took my bearings
        and checked my compass,
I was bending curve balls around the corner of July
or chasing two grey eyes,
that laughed at me from beneath dark gypsy curls.

Now, every time I pass a jukebox
        or turn on a radio,
I hear Willie Nelson singing
"Ain't It Funny How Time Slips Away".
Christ...
None of these DJ's ever heard of J.J.Cale
        "They Call Me the Breeze"?

One wrong turn,
coming out of Colorado,
blowing smoke to all four corners of the sky
        and a man winds up surrounded
by a pack of over-ripe evangelicals
beating Bibles into bayonets and breathing fire.

How the hell did I get here?
I swear I never saw that road sign
        never heard the warning horn,
just stepped out of the smoke and wreckage
and heard the siren's wail.

LETTING GO

Chronos and Inevitability have intertwined,
and there is no relief
in understanding the fading of a world
      circling a burning star.
There is no peace in loss
of self and soul wrapped in fleeting sands
that pour out like expelled air.

I miss the ache in my shoulder
after nine innings
of curve balls and cutters
      the leather smell
of a Wilson A2000, oiled
and placed on top of my spikes
in the bat bag.

I miss the salty taste of summer skin,
my lips pressing
the curve of your sweet belly
      July rain wearing the sky
like a white lace wedding veil
outside the rusted window screens
of 1976.

I miss Ralph Mooney's pedal steel
blending with Telecaster

This time will be the last time...
      Ladies Love Outlaws

eight track stereo rippling out windows
of a forest green Mercury Cougar
rolling over KATY tracks.

I miss the cackle and crow of roosters
in my father's barns
and him rocking beneath the elm
      Oklahoma drifting in
like a river mist, serene and certain,
air settling in the dusty aroma
of drying peanuts.

I miss Momma watering the purple
of four o'clocks
in the growing dusk before dark
      the full moon rising
to hang in the darkness
like a shining silver concho on the black
belt of night.

I miss brown-eyes behind a baseball bat,
sending tennis balls
deep beyond the limits of our backyard
      the little boy smile
before the becoming
of a master of chemistry
      in Colorado.

I have tried hard to release the years
      but I cannot,
although, I know a time will come
when all things end,
a time when worlds will spin into webs
      that wither in lost moments
dissolving in the mist of decades,
ephemeral and immeasurable, without bounds,
a final time for letting go

MICKEY MANTLE AND
CHINABERRY TREES

October descends
    like a feathering of dust
in an empty room,
and the color of fireflies fades
    from my summer nights
beneath a moon, alabaster white.

This cooling of air
    This shortening of the sun
has always bothered me.

I remember being ten,
sitting in the shade of a chinaberry tree
    grown to the fence
next to the house
where my grandmother lived
    before she didn't.

Rubbing Neatsfoot oil
into the laces
    the palm and the pocket
of my Rawlings baseball glove,
I remembered a Marty Robbins' song
drifting from the silent radio
    in a house that now stood empty.

The golden tan darkened
    around the X's
that stitched the fingers together
connecting pocket to thumb
    weaving a web of leather
designed to steal a baseball from the air.

Sometimes I can still see
the practiced cursive of Mickey Mantle
        etched into the palm
as my fingers measure the oil to rub
into the glove
        where his signature
is stamped like a cattle brand.

And if I try really hard
        half a century flown
like that great horned owl that haunts my dreams,
I can still smell the way the leather smelled
as I worked the oil
        meant for Dad's saddle
into the folds and crevices of that glove.

Long before I understood metaphor
or simile
        somehow
                even as a boy
when I leaned back against that chinaberry
and felt the rough bark through my sweatshirt,
I knew this season of coming beauty
        this time of turning leaves
marked endings I did not wish to see,
and I sensed a sadness
        that could not explain
watching the two kids next door throw a football
back and forth
        across the dying grass
                of their front lawn.

A FEW THINGS I'VE COME TO KNOW

Cowboys ride, painters paint
     curve balls break,
and Jimmy Buffett is still real cool.

Troubadours sing, bells ring
     horsepower always helps
and beer is best when served ice cold.

Drummers drum, buffalo roam
     children love to play
and ladies really do love outlaws.

Warriors fight, poets write
     pilgrims believe
and some men never change.

Mothers love, lovers touch
     flames burn
and broken hearts hurt like hell.

Worlds spin, words matter
     wounds can heal
and all too often heroes fail.

Baseballs bounce, gravity pulls
     brothers die
and time is running out.

THE COWBOY RIDES AWAY

(For Terry Ray)

I can't really remember your arrival.
    After all,
I was only three years and three months old.
But I knew who you were.
    You were a gift
        a nephew
            a little brother,
and a fireball cowboy to the core.

We ran.
    We played.
Hell, we even fought a time or two.

We watched over
our ever-expanding clan
    as other brothers came,
    sisters too.
We watched it break like shattered glass,
but we kept our hearts in place
    and always
had each other's backs.

When they told me you were gone
    anger roared
into my fractured heart
until I wiped my eyes and looked
out my window into a setting sun
    and saw you
sitting in the saddle of your
old paint pony,
    breathing easy,
untethered from tubes and tanks,
Oklahoma air filling both your lungs.
I saw your smiling eyes

peering out
from beneath a straw brim
        bent into a perfect curve.
You laughed
that I-got-away-with-something laugh of yours
and gave your horse a gentle nudge
off toward eternity.

        You knew full well
you weren't supposed to ride
before I did, and I was pissed,
but when you turned and waved goodbye
        I finally found a little peace
and forgave you for heading out so soon.

Afterall
        I should have known
you'd do things your own way
        you always did.
Sometimes
        I reckon,
a man's just gotta ride.

Terry Ray Risner 1957 -2023

ABOUT THE AUTHOR

R on Wallace is an Oklahoma native and currently an adjunct instructor of Literature at Southeastern Oklahoma State University, in Durant, Oklahoma. He is the author of eleven books of poetry, five of which have been finalists in the Oklahoma Book Awards.

Renegade and Other Poems was the 2018 winner of the Oklahoma Book Award. He has also edited *Bull Buffalo and Indian Paintbrush*, a collection of Oklahoma Poetry and completed his first novel, *A Secret Lies in New Orleans,* a finalist in fiction in the 2022 Oklahoma Book Awards. More of his work can be found at RonWallacePoetry.com